PROUDLY DESIGNED ON THE UPPER WEST SIDE
(OF KANSAS CITY).

TO BE READ UPON MY DEATH.*

*A SCANDALOUS MEMOIR ABOUT:

. . . .

YOURSELF

DISCLAIMER

× × ×

THINK OF THIS JOURNAL AS OUR LITTLE WAY OF TRYING TO GET PEOPLE TO BREAK OUT OF THEIR SHELL AND TELL PEOPLE ABOUT THEIR LIVES.

WE ALL LIVE AMAZING, COMPLEX, AND INCREDIBLY INTERESTING LIVES–AND ALL TOO OFTEN, WE JUST ASSUME THAT NO ONE ELSE REALLY WANTS TO HEAR ABOUT THEM. WELL, THAT COULDN'T BE FURTHER FROM THE TRUTH.

THIS JOURNAL WAS INSPIRED BY OUR CO-FOUNDER MELANIE. SHE OFTEN TALKED ABOUT WANTING TO TELL HER SON ABOUT ALL OF THE WILD THINGS THAT SHE HAD DONE IN HER LIFE–BUT LATER, YOU KNOW, SO THEY WOULDN'T GIVE HIM ANY 'INSPIRATION.' ANYWAY, WE FINALLY DECIDED TO MAKE IT POSSIBLE.

YES I KNOW, THAT LAST PARAGRAPH KIND OF SOUNDS LIKE MELANIE DIED. DON'T WORRY, SHE DIDN'T. SHE STILL HAS PLENTY OF TIME TO FILL OUT THE BOOK THAT SHE HELPED CREATE.

THAT SAID, DON'T TAKE THIS THING TOO LITERALLY. TELL YOUR STORIES–AND MODIFY THE PROMPTS AS NEEDED TO MAKE THEM MORE APPLICABLE TO YOUR LIFE. JUST PLEASE DON'T GO AND GET INSPIRED TO DO ANY (NEW) ILLEGAL THINGS–WE'RE NOT RESPONSIBLE IF YOU DO.

@ BRASSMONKEYGOODS

THIS JOURNAL IS DEDICATED
TO ALL OF OUR DECEASED FAMILY
MEMBERS. WE CAN ONLY IMAGINE
THE CRAZY STORIES THAT WE
NEVER GOT TO HEAR. ESPECIALLY
YOURS, DALE.

x x x

WE MISS YOU ALL.

HOW TO USE THIS BOOK

A TUTORIAL

OUR LIVES ARE ALL FILLED WITH AMAZING STORIES—THE JUICY ONES JUST MIGHT BETTER BE TOLD WHEN WE'RE DEAD.

THAT'S EXACTLY WHAT THIS JOURNAL IS FOR. ON THE FOLLOWING PAGES, YOU CAN SPILL THE BEANS ON ALL OF THE FUN AND/OR SLIGHTLY ILLEGAL THINGS THAT YOU'VE DONE IN YOUR LIFE—AND SHARE THEM WITH THE WORLD. LATER. YOU KNOW, WELL AFTER THE STATUTE OF LIMITATIONS.

SO JUST GO THROUGH THE BOOK AND USE THE PROVIDED PROMPTS TO RECALL ALL OF THE SORDID TALES OF YOUR PAST. YOU'LL PROBABLY BE SURPRISED AT ALL OF THE CRAZY THINGS THAT 'YOUNGER YOU' ACTUALLY DID. OKAY, BUT WHAT IF YOU DIDN'T ACTUALLY DO A FEW OF THEM? WELL, THAT SOUNDS LIKE A GREAT OPPORTUNITY AND/OR EXCUSE TO DO THEM NOW.*

JUST REMEMBER, THIS IS ALL IN GOOD FUN. WE'VE ALL DONE OUR FAIR SHARE OF QUESTIONABLE THINGS—EVEN WITH THE BEST OF INTENTIONS. SO JUST BECAUSE WE LISTED SOMETHING IN HERE DOESN'T MEAN IT'S ACTUALLY A GOOD IDEA—OR THAT WE'RE CONDONING IT IN ANY WAY.

IN OTHER WORDS, BE CAREFUL OUT THERE.

IN THE BACK OF THE BOOK, WE'VE ALSO PROVIDED YOU WITH A FEW SPACES TO ADD YOUR OWN 'CONFESSIONS'—PERFECT FOR TELLING YOUR OWN PERSONAL STORIES THAT ARE CRAZIER THAN WE COULD HAVE EVEN IMAGINED. PSST: IF YOU'RE BRAVE, GO AHEAD AND SHARE THEM WITH US AT @BRASSMONKEYGOODS. WE'D LOVE TO SEE THEM.

*REMEMBER THAT DISCLAIMER? WELL, IT'S BACK AGAIN: A PREREQUISITE HERE IS COMMON SENSE (AND A SENSE OF HUMOR). BY ALL MEANS TELL YOUR STORIES, JUST DON'T LET US INSPIRE YOU TO DO ANY (NEW) ILLEGAL ACTIVITIES—AND WE'RE NOT RESPONSIBLE IF YOU DO. WE WANT TO INSPIRE FUN, NOT LAWSUITS.

TO BE READ UPON MY DEATH • CONFESSION 1

ADULT THINGS THAT I STILL DON'T UNDERSTAND AS AN ACTUAL ADULT:

ANY REGRETS?

☐ YES

NOPE ☐

TO BE READ UPON MY DEATH • CONFESSION 2

I'LL NEVER BE ABLE TO UNSEE...

ANY REGRETS?

☐ YES

NOPE ☐

TO BE READ UPON MY DEATH • CONFESSION 3

HOW I'VE SUCCESSFULLY MADE IT THROUGH LIFE WITHOUT JOINING A STREET GANG:

ANY REGRETS?

☐ YES

NOPE ☐

TO BE READ UPON MY DEATH • CONFESSION 4

WHAT I LEARNED ABOUT FOOD POISONING DURING MY TRIP TO THE STATE FAIR:

ANY REGRETS?

☐ YES

NOPE ☐

WHAT FRIENDS, STRANGERS, AND POLICE REPORTS TELL ME ABOUT A CERTAIN (VERY DRUNK) NIGHT:

ANY REGRETS?

☐ YES

NOPE ☐

EXHIBIT A

I'M NOT A BURGLAR, BUT I DID ONCE BREAK INTO A...

ANY REGRETS?

☐ YES NOPE ☐

TO BE READ UPON MY DEATH • CONFESSION 7

THAT TIME I VOMITED, LIKE, A LOT:

ANY REGRETS?

☐ YES NOPE ☐

TO BE READ UPON MY DEATH • CONFESSION 8

MY FIRM STANCE ON THE USE OF PINEAPPLE AS A PIZZA TOPPING:

ANY REGRETS?

☐ YES NOPE ☐

TO BE READ UPON MY DEATH • CONFESSION 9

HOW I FOUND OUT THAT THE BACK SEAT OF A POLICE CAR IS SURPRISINGLY ROOMY:

ANY REGRETS?

☐ YES NOPE ☐

TO BE READ UPON MY DEATH • CONFESSION 10

THE HAPPIEST I'VE EVER BEEN (NOT NAKED):

ANY REGRETS?

☐ YES NOPE ☐

TO BE READ UPON MY DEATH • CONFESSION 11

LOOK, I'M NOT SAYING THAT I ONCE TRASHED A HOTEL ROOM, BUT...

. . . .

. . . .

. . . .

. . . .

. . . .

ANY REGRETS?

☐ YES NOPE ☐

TO BE READ UPON MY DEATH • CONFESSION 12

MY BIGGEST GUILTY PLEASURE:

. . . .

. . . .

. . . .

. . . .

. . . .

. . . .

ANY REGRETS?

☐ YES NOPE ☐

TO BE READ UPON MY DEATH • CONFESSION 13

MY HIGHLY CONTROVERSIAL FEELINGS ABOUT CILANTRO:

ANY REGRETS?

☐ YES NOPE ☐

TO BE READ UPON MY DEATH • CONFESSION 14

THE BEST EXCUSE I EVER USED TO GET OUT OF SCHOOL (AND WHAT I DID INSTEAD):

ANY REGRETS?

☐ YES NOPE ☐

THE TATTOO THAT NO ONE KNOWS I HAVE:

ANY REGRETS?

☐ YES NOPE ☐

EXHIBIT A

MY FAVORITE SCAR (AND HOW I GOT IT):

ANY REGRETS?

☐ YES NOPE ☐

EXHIBIT A

TO BE READ UPON MY DEATH • CONFESSION 17

THE DUMBEST THING I BELIEVED AS A CHILD:

ANY REGRETS?

☐ YES NOPE ☐

TO BE READ UPON MY DEATH • CONFESSION 18

THE ONE SONG THAT PRETTY MUCH SUMS UP HIGH SCHOOL FOR ME IS...

ANY REGRETS?

☐ YES NOPE ☐

TO BE READ UPON MY DEATH • CONFESSION 19

THE FIRST ALBUM THAT I EVER BOUGHT WAS:

ANY REGRETS?

☐ YES NOPE ☐

TO BE READ UPON MY DEATH • CONFESSION 20

HERE'S WHY YOU REALLY SHOULD REREAD EVERYTHING BEFORE YOU HIT SEND:

ANY REGRETS?

☐ YES NOPE ☐

TO BE READ UPON MY DEATH • CONFESSION 21

THAT ONE FASHION TREND THAT I REALLY WISH I HAD TAKEN A PASS ON:

ANY REGRETS?

☐ YES NOPE ☐

TO BE READ UPON MY DEATH • CONFESSION 22

THE BIGGEST THING THAT I EVER STOLE WAS:

ANY REGRETS?

☐ YES NOPE ☐

TO BE READ UPON MY DEATH • CONFESSION 23

AS IT TURNS OUT, NOT EVERYTHING YOU READ ON THE INTERNET IS TRUE:

ANY REGRETS?

☐ YES NOPE ☐

TO BE READ UPON MY DEATH • CONFESSION 24

THAT ONE TIME THAT MY CAR WAS BROKEN INTO AND ALL THEY TOOK WAS...

ANY REGRETS?

☐ YES NOPE ☐

THIS MOVIE NEVER FAILS TO MAKE ME CRY:

ANY REGRETS?

☐ YES NOPE ☐

EXHIBIT A

HANDS DOWN, THE MOST DISGUSTING BEVERAGE IN THE ENTIRE WORLD IS...

ANY REGRETS?

☐ YES

NOPE ☐

EXHIBIT A

TO BE READ UPON MY DEATH • CONFESSION 27

IN HINDSIGHT, I PROBABLY SHOULD HAVE JUST LEFT IT ALONE:

. . . .

. . . .

. . . .

. . . .

. . . .

ANY REGRETS?

☐ YES NOPE ☐

TO BE READ UPON MY DEATH • CONFESSION 28

MY PERSONAL BELIEFS IN REGARDS TO FOOD EXPIRATION DATES:

. . . .

. . . .

. . . .

. . . .

. . . .

ANY REGRETS?

☐ YES NOPE ☐

TO BE READ UPON MY DEATH • CONFESSION 29

HONESTLY, I BLAME AUTO CORRECT:

ANY REGRETS?

☐ YES NOPE ☐

TO BE READ UPON MY DEATH • CONFESSION 30

THAT TIME THAT I ACCIDENTALLY FOUND OUT I WAS DEATHLY ALLERGIC TO...

ANY REGRETS?

☐ YES NOPE ☐

TO BE READ UPON MY DEATH • CONFESSION 31

THE BEST BOOK EVER WRITTEN (ACCORDING TO ME):

ANY REGRETS?

☐ YES NOPE ☐

TO BE READ UPON MY DEATH • CONFESSION 32

THE MOST ANNOYING BOSS I EVER HAD:

ANY REGRETS?

☐ YES NOPE ☐

WHAT I WISH I HAD KNOWN ABOUT BUYING A HOUSE BEFORE I BOUGHT ONE:

ANY REGRETS?

☐ YES NOPE ☐

EXHIBIT A

THAT TIME THAT I PRETENDED LIKE I KNEW WHAT I WAS DOING—EVEN THOUGH I DIDN'T HAVE A CLUE:

ANY REGRETS?

☐ YES NOPE ☐

TO BE READ UPON MY DEATH • CONFESSION 35

IF I WERE TO PUT A CELEBRITY IN MY WILL, IT WOULD OBVIOUSLY HAVE TO BE...

ANY REGRETS?

☐ YES NOPE ☐

TO BE READ UPON MY DEATH • CONFESSION 36

MY STANCE ON THE USE OF RAISINS IN COOKIES:

ANY REGRETS?

☐ YES NOPE ☐

GROWING UP, I WAS ABSOLUTELY POSITIVE THAT I WAS GOING TO BECOME A...

ANY REGRETS?

☐ YES

NOPE ☐

EXHIBIT A

I HAVE YET TO CONFIRM THIS WITH A THERAPIST, BUT I'M PRETTY SURE I WAS SCARRED FOR LIFE BY...

ANY REGRETS?

☐ YES

NOPE ☐

TO BE READ UPON MY DEATH • CONFESSION 39

MY STANCE ON WAFFLES VS. PANCAKES:

ANY REGRETS?

☐ YES NOPE ☐

TO BE READ UPON MY DEATH • CONFESSION 40

AS IT TURNS OUT, I SHOULDN'T HAVE GOTTEN THAT PIERCING:

ANY REGRETS?

☐ YES NOPE ☐

TO BE READ UPON MY DEATH • CONFESSION 41

THAT ONE TIME THAT I MANAGED TO SNEAK BACKSTAGE (AND WHY IT WAS TOTALLY WORTH IT):

ANY REGRETS?

☐ YES

NOPE ☐

TO BE READ UPON MY DEATH • CONFESSION 42

IT WOULD ONLY BE FITTING IF MY ASHES WERE STORED IN A:

ANY REGRETS?

☐ YES

NOPE ☐

TO BE READ UPON MY DEATH • CONFESSION 43

LET ME TELL YOU SOMETHING ABOUT BIRDS:

ANY REGRETS?

☐ YES NOPE ☐

TO BE READ UPON MY DEATH • CONFESSION 44

LET ME TELL YOU SOMETHING ABOUT BEES:

ANY REGRETS?

☐ YES NOPE ☐

TO BE READ UPON MY DEATH • CONFESSION 45

THAT TIME THAT I DECIDED TO RUN A MARATHON (AND WHY MY LEGS NEVER FELT NORMAL AGAIN):

ANY REGRETS?

☐ YES NOPE ☐

TO BE READ UPON MY DEATH • CONFESSION 46

UM, NOT TO BRAG, BUT I ONCE WON A MAJOR AWARD:

ANY REGRETS?

☐ YES NOPE ☐

MY SECRET TALENT IS...

ANY REGRETS?

☐ YES NOPE ☐

EXHIBIT A

MY PROUDEST MOMENT WAS...

ANY REGRETS?

☐ YES NOPE ☐

EXHIBIT A

TO BE READ UPON MY DEATH • CONFESSION 49

A CAUTIONARY TALE ABOUT BUYING USED SHOES:

ANY REGRETS?

☐ YES NOPE ☐

TO BE READ UPON MY DEATH • CONFESSION 50

THERE SHOULD DEFINITELY BE A NATIONAL HOLIDAY TO CELEBRATE...

ANY REGRETS?

☐ YES NOPE ☐

TO BE READ UPON MY DEATH • CONFESSION 51

THAT ONE TIME I FELT LIKE I WAS FAMOUS:

ANY REGRETS?

☐ YES NOPE ☐

TO BE READ UPON MY DEATH • CONFESSION 52

I ALWAYS SMILE WHEN I THINK ABOUT:

ANY REGRETS?

☐ YES NOPE ☐

TO BE READ UPON MY DEATH • CONFESSION 53

THE LONGEST THAT I HAVE EVER STAYED AWAKE (WITH OR WITHOUT CAFFEINE):

ANY REGRETS?

☐ YES NOPE ☐

TO BE READ UPON MY DEATH • CONFESSION 54

THE LONGEST THAT I'VE EVER SLEPT (NOT INCLUDING BATHROOM BREAKS):

ANY REGRETS?

☐ YES NOPE ☐

TO BE READ UPON MY DEATH • CONFESSION 55

I'VE NEVER LOVED TO HATE SOMEONE MORE THAN...

ANY REGRETS?

☐ YES

NOPE ☐

TO BE READ UPON MY DEATH • CONFESSION 56

I'VE NEVER HATED TO LOVE SOMEONE MORE THAN...

ANY REGRETS?

☐ YES

NOPE ☐

HORROR MOVIES HAVE IT ALL WRONG BECAUSE THERE'S NOTHING MORE TERRIFYING THAN:

ANY REGRETS?

☐ YES NOPE ☐

EXHIBIT A

I NEVER THROW UP ON THEME PARK RIDES—EXCEPT FOR THAT TIME I...

ANY REGRETS?

☐ YES NOPE ☐

EXHIBIT A

TO BE READ UPON MY DEATH • CONFESSION 59

THE NIGHT I WAS GLAD THAT ATMs EXIST:

ANY REGRETS?

☐ YES NOPE ☐

TO BE READ UPON MY DEATH • CONFESSION 60

MY VERDICT ON SMOOTH VS. CHUNKY PEANUT BUTTER:

ANY REGRETS?

☐ YES NOPE ☐

TO BE READ UPON MY DEATH • CONFESSION 61

I THINK I'M ONLY TRULY HAPPY WHEN...

ANY REGRETS?

☐ YES NOPE ☐

TO BE READ UPON MY DEATH • CONFESSION 62

SOME PEOPLE ARGUE THAT 'DIE HARD' IS A CHRISTMAS MOVIE—AND I SAY THOSE PEOPLE ARE...

ANY REGRETS?

☐ YES NOPE ☐

TO BE READ UPON MY DEATH • CONFESSION 63

THE FIRST TIME THAT I RAN OUT OF GAS (AND IN NO WAY LEARNED ANY KIND OF LESSON FROM IT):

. . . .

. . . .

. . . .

. . . .

. . . .

ANY REGRETS?

☐ YES NOPE ☐

TO BE READ UPON MY DEATH • CONFESSION 64

I SWEAR, I THOUGHT I WAS ON MUTE:

. . . .

. . . .

. . . .

. . . .

. . . .

. . . .

ANY REGRETS?

☐ YES NOPE ☐

THE MOMENT THAT I REALIZED BRUCE WILLIS WAS ACTUALLY DEAD THE WHOLE TIME:

ANY REGRETS?

☐ YES NOPE ☐

I COULD WRITE AN ENTIRE BOOK (IF NOT A 10-VOLUME SERIES) ABOUT:

ANY REGRETS?

☐ YES NOPE ☐

I WISH SOMEBODY HAD TOLD ME...

ANY REGRETS?

☐ YES

NOPE ☐

EXHIBIT A

I THINK IT WAS SOME SORT OF SIGN...

ANY REGRETS?

☐ YES NOPE ☐

EXHIBIT A

TO BE READ UPON MY DEATH • CONFESSION 69

THAT ONE TIME THAT I PROBABLY SHOULD HAVE GONE TO THE DOCTOR WAY EARLIER:

. . . .

. . . .

. . . .

. . . .

. . . .

ANY REGRETS?

☐ YES NOPE ☐

TO BE READ UPON MY DEATH • CONFESSION 70

WHEN IT COMES TO DRIVING, I CONSIDER MYSELF...

. . . .

. . . .

. . . .

. . . .

. . . .

ANY REGRETS?

☐ YES NOPE ☐

TO BE READ UPON MY DEATH • CONFESSION 71

I ADMIRE MY MOM MOST FOR...

ANY REGRETS?

☐ YES NOPE ☐

TO BE READ UPON MY DEATH • CONFESSION 72

I STILL DON'T KNOW HOW MY DAD...

ANY REGRETS?

☐ YES NOPE ☐

TO BE READ UPON MY DEATH • CONFESSION 73

YOU PROBABLY ALREADY KNOW THIS, BUT MY BIGGEST PET PEEVE IS...

ANY REGRETS?

☐ YES NOPE ☐

TO BE READ UPON MY DEATH • CONFESSION 74

THAT ONE TIME THAT I WAS ALMOST THROWN OUT OF A COUNTRY:

ANY REGRETS?

☐ YES NOPE ☐

TO BE READ UPON MY DEATH • CONFESSION 75

MY WORST SUBJECT IN SCHOOL WAS...

. . . .

. . . .

. . . .

. . . .

. . . .

. . . .

ANY REGRETS?

☐ YES NOPE ☐

TO BE READ UPON MY DEATH • CONFESSION 76

MY BEST SUBJECT IN SCHOOL WAS...

. . . .

. . . .

. . . .

. . . .

. . . .

. . . .

ANY REGRETS?

☐ YES NOPE ☐

IGNORE MY FULL BAR AND WINE RACK, MY FIRST LEGIT ADDICTION WAS...

ANY REGRETS?

☐ YES

NOPE ☐

EXHIBIT A

I'VE HAD SOME PRETTY BAD BREAKUPS, BUT THE WORST ONE BY FAR WAS...

ANY REGRETS?

☐ YES NOPE ☐

TO BE READ UPON MY DEATH • CONFESSION 79

THERE'S NO QUESTION ABOUT IT, MY FAVORITE HOLIDAY HAS ALWAYS BEEN:

ANY REGRETS?

☐ YES

NOPE ☐

TO BE READ UPON MY DEATH • CONFESSION 80

THE NICEST THING THAT I'VE EVER DONE—AND DIDN'T TELL ANYONE ABOUT (SO IT ACTUALLY COUNTS):

ANY REGRETS?

☐ YES

NOPE ☐

TO BE READ UPON MY DEATH • CONFESSION 81

IF MY LIFE BECAME A MAJOR MOTION PICTURE, THE STARRING ROLE SHOULD OBVIOUSLY BE PLAYED BY...

ANY REGRETS?

☐ YES NOPE ☐

TO BE READ UPON MY DEATH • CONFESSION 82

THE DAY I LEARNED SANTA CLAUS WASN'T REAL AND REALITY AS I KNEW IT CRUMBLED AROUND ME:

ANY REGRETS?

☐ YES NOPE ☐

TO BE READ UPON MY DEATH • CONFESSION 83

THE FIRST JOB I EVER HAD:

ANY REGRETS?

☐ YES NOPE ☐

TO BE READ UPON MY DEATH • CONFESSION 84

THE FIRST JOB I WAS EVER FIRED FROM:

ANY REGRETS?

☐ YES NOPE ☐

TO BE READ UPON MY DEATH • CONFESSION 85

THE ONE PLACE THAT I SHOULD PROBABLY NEVER GO BACK TO (OR THEY WILL LIKELY PRESS CHARGES)...

ANY REGRETS?

☐ YES NOPE ☐

TO BE READ UPON MY DEATH • CONFESSION 86

AN HONEST REVIEW OF THE TIME(S) THAT I WENT SKINNY DIPPING:

ANY REGRETS?

☐ YES NOPE ☐

IT WAS A DAY THAT I'LL NEVER FORGET...

ANY REGRETS?

☐ YES NOPE ☐

EXHIBIT A

WE ALL KNOW THE BEST JAMES BOND WAS:

ANY REGRETS?

☐ YES NOPE ☐

EXHIBIT A

TO BE READ UPON MY DEATH • CONFESSION 89

TO THIS DAY, MY PARENTS (THANKFULLY) STILL DON'T KNOW ABOUT THE TIME THAT I...

ANY REGRETS?

☐ YES NOPE ☐

TO BE READ UPON MY DEATH • CONFESSION 90

I HONESTLY THINK I WAS BORN IN THE WRONG DECADE (AND HERE'S WHY):

ANY REGRETS?

☐ YES NOPE ☐

TO BE READ UPON MY DEATH • CONFESSION 91

THE FIRST CONCERT I WENT TO WAS:

ANY REGRETS?

☐ YES NOPE ☐

TO BE READ UPON MY DEATH • CONFESSION 92

THE FIRST CONCERT I WENT TO THAT I'M NOT EMBARRASSED BY WAS:

ANY REGRETS?

☐ YES NOPE ☐

TO BE READ UPON MY DEATH • CONFESSION 93

THAT TIME THAT MY FAVORITE SONG IN THE WORLD WAS RUINED FOREVER THANKS TO...

ANY REGRETS?

☐ YES NOPE ☐

TO BE READ UPON MY DEATH • CONFESSION 94

I'VE NEVER HATED A SONG MORE THAN...

ANY REGRETS?

☐ YES NOPE ☐

TO BE READ UPON MY DEATH • CONFESSION 95

I HAVE TO GIVE THEM CREDIT, MY PARENTS AT LEAST GOT ONE THING RIGHT:

ANY REGRETS?

☐ YES

NOPE ☐

TO BE READ UPON MY DEATH • CONFESSION 96

AS IT TURNS OUT, YOU REALLY DO HAVE TO PAY TAXES:

ANY REGRETS?

☐ YES

NOPE ☐

THE BEST CAR I'VE EVER OWNED WAS...

ANY REGRETS?

☐ YES

NOPE ☐

EXHIBIT A

I AM TOTALLY CONVINCED THAT IN A PREVIOUS LIFE I HAD TO HAVE BEEN A...

ANY REGRETS?

☐ YES

NOPE ☐

EXHIBIT A

TO BE READ UPON MY DEATH • CONFESSION 99

MY BEST TRAIT IS (PROBABLY)...

ANY REGRETS?

☐ YES NOPE ☐

TO BE READ UPON MY DEATH • CONFESSION 100

MY WORST TRAIT IS (CERTAINLY)...

ANY REGRETS?

☐ YES NOPE ☐

TO BE READ UPON MY DEATH • CONFESSION 101

IF I HAD A SIGNATURE COCKTAIL IT WOULD BE:

ANY REGRETS?

☐ YES NOPE ☐

TO BE READ UPON MY DEATH • CONFESSION 102

IN MY OPINION, THERE'S ONLY ONE CORRECT WAY TO PRONOUNCE 'AUNT' AND IT'S...

ANY REGRETS?

☐ YES NOPE ☐

TO BE READ UPON MY DEATH • CONFESSION 103

THEY DON'T TEACH THIS IN SCHOOL (BUT IT WOULD BE REALLY HELPFUL IF THEY DID):

ANY REGRETS?

☐ YES NOPE ☐

TO BE READ UPON MY DEATH • CONFESSION 104

OK, I'M A LITTLE TOO PASSIONATE ABOUT...

ANY REGRETS?

☐ YES NOPE ☐

THE WILDEST THING I'VE EVER DONE WHILE (ALLEGEDLY) INTOXICATED:

ANY REGRETS?

☐ YES NOPE ☐

EXHIBIT A

THE WILDEST THING I'VE EVER DONE SOBER (AND HAVE ABSOLUTELY NO EXCUSE FOR):

ANY REGRETS?

☐ YES

NOPE ☐

TO BE READ UPON MY DEATH • CONFESSION 107

AND ON THAT NIGHT, I TRULY LEARNED WHY THEY CALL IT GAMBLING:

ANY REGRETS?

☐ YES NOPE ☐

TO BE READ UPON MY DEATH • CONFESSION 108

I'LL NEVER FORGET THE DAY THAT I FOUND OUT PAUL NEWMAN MADE MOVIES BEFORE SALAD DRESSING:

ANY REGRETS?

☐ YES NOPE ☐

NOW THAT I HAVE SOME TIME AND DISTANCE, I CLEARLY OVERPAID FOR...

ANY REGRETS?

☐ YES NOPE ☐

EXHIBIT A

DEFINITIVE PROOF THAT THE MOST OVERRATED THING IN LIFE IS:

ANY REGRETS?

☐ YES

NOPE ☐

TO BE READ UPON MY DEATH • CONFESSION 111

MY BEST FRIEND GROWING UP WAS...

ANY REGRETS?

☐ YES NOPE ☐

TO BE READ UPON MY DEATH • CONFESSION 112

MY 15 MINUTES OF FAME—AND HOW IT MOLDED ME INTO THE STAR YOU KNOW TODAY:

ANY REGRETS?

☐ YES NOPE ☐

TO BE READ UPON MY DEATH • CONFESSION 113

I WISH I WAS MAKING THIS UP, BUT I STILL GET PHYSICALLY ILL AT THE SMELL OF...

ANY REGRETS?

☐ YES NOPE ☐

TO BE READ UPON MY DEATH • CONFESSION 114

I'LL NEVER FORGET MY FIRST...

ANY REGRETS?

☐ YES NOPE ☐

TO BE READ UPON MY DEATH • CONFESSION 115

MY MOST RIDICULOUS AND LONGEST STANDING SUPERSTITION (THAT I WILL ALWAYS CONTINUE TO HAVE):

ANY REGRETS?

☐ YES NOPE ☐

TO BE READ UPON MY DEATH • CONFESSION 116

THE BEST FIVE DOLLARS I EVER SPENT:

ANY REGRETS?

☐ YES NOPE ☐

TO BE READ UPON MY DEATH • CONFESSION 117

YOU KNOW, I REALLY THOUGHT I WAS DYING—BUT IT TURNS OUT THAT IT WAS JUST...

ANY REGRETS?

☐ YES NOPE ☐

TO BE READ UPON MY DEATH • CONFESSION 118

EVEN THOUGH NO ONE WILL BELIEVE ME, I STILL CAN'T EXPLAIN WHAT I SAW (*COUGH* ALIENS *COUGH*):

ANY REGRETS?

☐ YES NOPE ☐

MY FAVORITE SWEAR WORDS, IN ORDER:

ANY REGRETS?

☐ YES NOPE ☐

EXHIBIT A

THE SCARIEST MOMENT OF MY LIFE WAS...

ANY REGRETS?

☐ YES NOPE ☐

EXHIBIT A

TO BE READ UPON MY DEATH • CONFESSION 121

IN HINDSIGHT, I PROBABLY SHOULDN'T HAVE PUT THAT IN MY MOUTH:

ANY REGRETS?

☐ YES NOPE ☐

TO BE READ UPON MY DEATH • CONFESSION 122

FOR BETTER OR FOR WORSE, HERE'S WHY I'LL NEVER, EVER FORGET HIGH SCHOOL:

ANY REGRETS?

☐ YES NOPE ☐

TO BE READ UPON MY DEATH • CONFESSION 123

MY LIFE DESCRIBED IN MOVIE QUOTES:

ANY REGRETS?

☐ YES

NOPE ☐

TO BE READ UPON MY DEATH • CONFESSION 124

I HAVE AN OPEN MIND—EXCEPT FOR MY OPINION ON WHETHER OR NOT A HOT DOG IS A SANDWICH:

ANY REGRETS?

☐ YES

NOPE ☐

TO BE READ UPON MY DEATH • CONFESSION 125

AS IT TURNS OUT, YOU CAN ACTUALLY BUY HAPPINESS AT:

ANY REGRETS?

☐ YES NOPE ☐

TO BE READ UPON MY DEATH • CONFESSION 126

MY BIGGEST GUILTY PLEASURE:

ANY REGRETS?

☐ YES NOPE ☐

TO BE READ UPON MY DEATH • CONFESSION 127

I PROMISE THIS STORY IS 100% TRUE—AND YET NO ONE HAS EVER BELIEVED ME:

ANY REGRETS?

☐ YES NOPE ☐

TO BE READ UPON MY DEATH • CONFESSION 128

I'M NOT PROUD TO ADMIT IT, BUT I HATED THEM FROM THE MOMENT I MET THEM...

ANY REGRETS?

☐ YES NOPE ☐

MY STANCE ON PENS VS. PENCILS:

ANY REGRETS?

☐ YES

NOPE ☐

EXHIBIT A

TO BE READ UPON MY DEATH • CONFESSION 130

THE DUMBEST HOLIDAY HAS TO BE...

ANY REGRETS?

☐ YES   NOPE ☐

TO BE READ UPON MY DEATH • CONFESSION 131

A CAUTIONARY TALE ABOUT WHY YOU SHOULD ALWAYS CLEAR YOUR SEARCH HISTORY:

ANY REGRETS?

☐ YES   NOPE ☐

TO BE READ UPON MY DEATH • CONFESSION 132

SERIOUSLY, I MUST HAVE MISSED SCHOOL THE DAY THAT THEY EXPLAINED...

ANY REGRETS?

☐ YES

NOPE ☐

TO BE READ UPON MY DEATH • CONFESSION 133

I'M STILL NOT SURE WHY IT'S ILLEGAL, BUT...

ANY REGRETS?

☐ YES

NOPE ☐

TO BE READ UPON MY DEATH • CONFESSION 134

MY DEEPLY-HELD PERSONAL BELIEFS IN REGARDS TO ROCK CANDY:

ANY REGRETS?

☐ YES NOPE ☐

TO BE READ UPON MY DEATH • CONFESSION 135

THE ONE THING THAT I COULDN'T LIVE WITHOUT (YOU KNOW, BESIDES FOOD AND WATER):

ANY REGRETS?

☐ YES NOPE ☐

THE EXACT MOMENT I REALIZED I WAS OLD:

ANY REGRETS?

☐ YES NOPE ☐

EXHIBIT A

I ABSOLUTELY WASN'T READY FOR...

ANY REGRETS?

☐ YES NOPE ☐

EXHIBIT A

TO BE READ UPON MY DEATH • CONFESSION 138

ONE OF THE MANY TIMES THAT I PROBABLY SHOULD HAVE DIED:

TO BE READ UPON MY DEATH • CONFESSION 139

AS IT TURNS OUT, PEOPLE CAN STILL SEE YOU EVEN IF YOU CAN'T SEE THEM...

TO BE READ UPON MY DEATH • CONFESSION 140

MY FIRM STANCE ON CLOWNS:

ANY REGRETS?

☐ YES

NOPE ☐

TO BE READ UPON MY DEATH • CONFESSION 141

HOW I MANAGED TO STAY AWAY FROM DRUGS MY ENTIRE LIFE AND LEAD A CLEAN AND SOBER LIFE (JK, NOT REALLY):

ANY REGRETS?

☐ YES

NOPE ☐

TO BE READ UPON MY DEATH • CONFESSION 142

ONE OF THE MANY REASONS WHY YOU SHOULDN'T BUY GROCERY STORE SUSHI:

ANY REGRETS?

☐ YES NOPE ☐

TO BE READ UPON MY DEATH • CONFESSION 143

I WOULDN'T CALL MYSELF A HERO, BUT...

ANY REGRETS?

☐ YES NOPE ☐

TO BE READ UPON MY DEATH • CONFESSION 144

THE BIGGEST MISTAKE OF MY LIFE (THAT TURNED OUT GREAT):

ANY REGRETS?

☐ YES NOPE ☐

TO BE READ UPON MY DEATH • CONFESSION 145

THE BIGGEST MISTAKE OF MY LIFE (LIKE, FOR REAL):

ANY REGRETS?

☐ YES NOPE ☐

WELL, I CAN LAUGH AT IT NOW, BUT BARELY:

ANY REGRETS?

☐ YES NOPE ☐

EXHIBIT A

I GUESS I WAS A LITTLE OVERCONFIDENT IN MY SUBWAY NAVIGATING ABILITIES...

ANY REGRETS?

☐ YES

NOPE ☐

EXHIBIT A

TO BE READ UPON MY DEATH • CONFESSION 148

IN HINDSIGHT, IT WAS THE BEST JOB EVER:

ANY REGRETS?

☐ YES NOPE ☐

TO BE READ UPON MY DEATH • CONFESSION 149

IT WAS IMMEDIATELY APPARENT THAT I MADE A HUGE MISTAKE WHEN I TOOK THAT JOB:

ANY REGRETS?

☐ YES NOPE ☐

TO BE READ UPON MY DEATH • CONFESSION 150

MY MOST PROFOUND PIECE OF ADVICE IS:

ANY REGRETS?

☐ YES NOPE ☐

TO BE READ UPON MY DEATH • CONFESSION 151

MY LEAST PROFOUND PIECE OF ADVICE IS:

ANY REGRETS?

☐ YES NOPE ☐

TO BE READ UPON MY DEATH • CONFESSION 152

THAT TIME I WAS STUCK IN THE AIRPORT FOR SO LONG, I STARTED TO THINK THAT I LIVED THERE:

ANY REGRETS?

☐ YES NOPE ☐

TO BE READ UPON MY DEATH • CONFESSION 153

THE CLOSEST THAT I'VE EVER COME TO BELIEVING IN GHOSTS WAS WHEN...

ANY REGRETS?

☐ YES NOPE ☐

THAT TIME I WAS TRAPPED IN AN ELEVATOR—AND IT WAS DEFINITELY NOT CUTE LIKE A ROM-COM:

ANY REGRETS?

☐ YES NOPE ☐

THE FAMILY PET THAT I LOVED MORE THAN MOST OF MY BLOOD RELATIVES:

ANY REGRETS?

☐ YES NOPE ☐

IT'S A LONG DRIVE, BUT TOTALLY WORTH IT:

ANY REGRETS?

☐ YES NOPE ☐

EXHIBIT A

THE HARDEST THING I'VE EVER HAD TO DO:

ANY REGRETS?

☐ YES NOPE ☐

EXHIBIT A

TO BE READ UPON MY DEATH • CONFESSION 158

A CAUTIONARY TALE ABOUT PICKING ON YOUR SIBLINGS (NO MATTER HOW FEEBLE THEY LOOK):

ANY REGRETS?

☐ YES   NOPE ☐

TO BE READ UPON MY DEATH • CONFESSION 159

I HADN'T ACTUALLY PLANNED ON SWIMMING THAT DAY, BUT LIFE HAD OTHER PLANS:

ANY REGRETS?

☐ YES   NOPE ☐

TO BE READ UPON MY DEATH • CONFESSION 160

WHY YOU SHOULDN'T GO ON BLIND DATES:

ANY REGRETS?

☐ YES NOPE ☐

TO BE READ UPON MY DEATH • CONFESSION 161

A CAUTIONARY TALE ABOUT SHOPPING ONLINE WHILE YOU'RE DRUNK:

ANY REGRETS?

☐ YES NOPE ☐

TO BE READ UPON MY DEATH • CONFESSION 162

I'M NOT SAYING I WAS ABDUCTED BY ALIENS, BUT HOW ELSE DO YOU EXPLAIN THIS:

ANY REGRETS?

☐ YES NOPE ☐

TO BE READ UPON MY DEATH • CONFESSION 163

MY STANCE ON WHITE VS. DARK CHOCOLATE:

ANY REGRETS?

☐ YES NOPE ☐

TO BE READ UPON MY DEATH • CONFESSION 164

THE FIRST TIME I DROVE A CAR:

ANY REGRETS?

☐ YES NOPE ☐

TO BE READ UPON MY DEATH • CONFESSION 165

THE FIRST TIME I WRECKED A CAR:

ANY REGRETS?

☐ YES NOPE ☐

THE APPROXIMATE TIMELINE OF MY ACCEPTANCE OF VARIOUS VEGETABLES:

ANY REGRETS?

☐ YES

NOPE ☐

EXHIBIT A

IT (PROBABLY) WASN'T BEANIE BABIES, BUT I STILL WASTED SO MUCH OF MY MONEY COLLECTING...

ANY REGRETS?

☐ YES NOPE ☐

EXHIBIT A

TO BE READ UPON MY DEATH • CONFESSION 168

WHY YOU SHOULD ALWAYS SAVE THE RECEIPT:

ANY REGRETS?

☐ YES NOPE ☐

TO BE READ UPON MY DEATH • CONFESSION 169

THE NIGHT I SPENT IN THE E.R. (AND HOW MANY YEARS IT TOOK ME TO PAY THE BILL):

ANY REGRETS?

☐ YES NOPE ☐

TO BE READ UPON MY DEATH • CONFESSION 170

THE DAY I LEARNED WHAT A SUBPOENA WAS:

. . . .

. . . .

. . . .

. . . .

. . . .

. . . .

ANY REGRETS?

☐ YES NOPE ☐

TO BE READ UPON MY DEATH • CONFESSION 171

THE 'HARMLESS' CHILDREN'S MOVIE THAT ABSOLUTELY SCARRED ME FOR LIFE:

. . . .

. . . .

. . . .

. . . .

. . . .

ANY REGRETS?

☐ YES NOPE ☐

TO BE READ UPON MY DEATH • CONFESSION 172

THE BEST PLACE I EVER LIVED WAS:

ANY REGRETS?

☐ YES NOPE ☐

TO BE READ UPON MY DEATH • CONFESSION 173

THE WORST PLACE I EVER LIVED WAS:

ANY REGRETS?

☐ YES NOPE ☐

IF I HAD ALL THE MONEY IN THE WORLD AND COULD LIVE ANYWHERE, IT WOULD ABSOLUTELY BE...

ANY REGRETS?

☐ YES　　NOPE ☐

EXHIBIT A

READING THIS MEANS YOU ARE NOW COMPLICIT & SWORN TO SECRECY BECAUSE NOBODY KNOWS THAT I ONCE...

ANY REGRETS?

☐ YES NOPE ☐

TO BE READ UPON MY DEATH • CONFESSION 176

IT SEEMED LIKE A GOOD IDEA AT THE TIME...

. . . .

. . . .

. . . .

. . . .

. . . .

. . . .

ANY REGRETS?

☐ YES NOPE ☐

TO BE READ UPON MY DEATH • CONFESSION 177

WHAT I WAS PROBABLY DOING WHEN I SHOULD HAVE BEEN IN HIGH SCHOOL:

. . . .

. . . .

. . . .

. . . .

. . . .

ANY REGRETS?

☐ YES NOPE ☐

OUR STRANGEST FAMILY HEIRLOOM (THAT MAY OR MAY NOT BE HAUNTED):

ANY REGRETS?

☐ YES

NOPE ☐

EXHIBIT A

HERE'S WHY YOU SHOULDN'T GO TO YOUR OFFICE HOLIDAY PARTY (DESPITE THE FREE FOOD AND BOOZE):

ANY REGRETS?

☐ YES

NOPE ☐

TO BE READ UPON MY DEATH • CONFESSION 180

THE CLASS THAT CHANGED MY LIFE:

ANY REGRETS?

☐ YES NOPE ☐

TO BE READ UPON MY DEATH • CONFESSION 181

THEY SEEM CUTE AND INNOCENT, BUT LET ME TELL YOU SOMETHING ABOUT SQUIRRELS:

ANY REGRETS?

☐ YES NOPE ☐

TO BE READ UPON MY DEATH • CONFESSION 182

THE SECURITY DEPOSIT I NEVER SAW AGAIN (AND WHY IT WAS TOTALLY WORTH IT):

ANY REGRETS?

☐ YES NOPE ☐

TO BE READ UPON MY DEATH • CONFESSION 183

ADVICE I WOULD GIVE MY 18-YEAR-OLD SELF:

ANY REGRETS?

☐ YES NOPE ☐

TO BE READ UPON MY DEATH • CONFESSION 184

THE WORST PRESENT I EVER RECEIVED:

ANY REGRETS?

☐ YES NOPE ☐

TO BE READ UPON MY DEATH • CONFESSION 185

THE WORST PRESENT I EVER GAVE:

ANY REGRETS?

☐ YES NOPE ☐

TO BE READ UPON MY DEATH • CONFESSION 186

THAT TIME I WAS BUMPED UP TO FIRST CLASS (AND HOW THE REST OF MY LIFE WAS RUINED):

ANY REGRETS?

☐ YES NOPE ☐

TO BE READ UPON MY DEATH • CONFESSION 187

IN HINDSIGHT, I DEFINITELY SHOULD HAVE BOUGHT THE EXTENDED WARRANTY:

ANY REGRETS?

☐ YES NOPE ☐

THE BEST BAR IN THE WHOLE WORLD IS...

ANY REGRETS?

☐ YES NOPE ☐

EXHIBIT A

MY MOST UNLIKELY FRIEND WAS...

ANY REGRETS?

☐ YES NOPE ☐

EXHIBIT A

TO BE READ UPON MY DEATH • CONFESSION 190

HATE IS A STRONG WORD THAT YOU SHOULDN'T USE LIGHTLY—AND I REALLY HATED THAT GUY:

ANY REGRETS?

☐ YES NOPE ☐

TO BE READ UPON MY DEATH • CONFESSION 191

I COULD PROBABLY EAT THIS EVERY DAY FOR THE REST OF MY LIFE AND NEVER GET SICK OF IT:

ANY REGRETS?

☐ YES NOPE ☐

TO BE READ UPON MY DEATH • CONFESSION 192

THE TIME I WAS MISTAKEN FOR A CELEBRITY:

ANY REGRETS?

☐ YES NOPE ☐

TO BE READ UPON MY DEATH • CONFESSION 193

THE PRECISE MOMENT THAT I REALIZED THAT I HAD NO IDEA HOW TO FIGHT:

ANY REGRETS?

☐ YES NOPE ☐

TO BE READ UPON MY DEATH • CONFESSION 194

EVEN BEAR GRYLLS WOULD HAVE BEEN IMPRESSED BY HOW LOST THAT I MANAGED TO GET:

ANY REGRETS?

☐ YES

NOPE ☐

TO BE READ UPON MY DEATH • CONFESSION 195

MY STANCE ON BREAKFAST FOR DINNER:

ANY REGRETS?

☐ YES

NOPE ☐

TO BE READ UPON MY DEATH • CONFESSION 196

THE MOST DISGUSTING FOOD IN THE WORLD (ACCORDING TO ME):

ANY REGRETS?

☐ YES NOPE ☐

TO BE READ UPON MY DEATH • CONFESSION 197

IN RETROSPECT, I'M NOT SURE HOW I DIDN'T SEE ALL OF THOSE RED FLAGS:

ANY REGRETS?

☐ YES NOPE ☐

THE MOST TOURISTY THING I'VE EVER DONE:

ANY REGRETS?

☐ YES NOPE ☐

EXHIBIT A

I QUICKLY LEARNED THAT YOU'RE NOT ACTUALLY ALLOWED TO DO THAT IN PUBLIC:

ANY REGRETS?

☐ YES

NOPE ☐

EXHIBIT A

TO BE READ UPON MY DEATH • CONFESSION 200

I NEEDED A VACATION AFTER THAT VACATION:

ANY REGRETS?

☐ YES NOPE ☐

TO BE READ UPON MY DEATH • CONFESSION 201

MY STANCE ON AMERICAN CHEESE (AND OTHER CHEESE-LIKE PRODUCTS):

ANY REGRETS?

☐ YES NOPE ☐

TO BE READ UPON MY DEATH • CONFESSION 202

THE YEAR THAT EVERYTHING WENT RIGHT:

ANY REGRETS?

☐ YES NOPE ☐

TO BE READ UPON MY DEATH • CONFESSION 203

THE YEAR THAT EVERYTHING WENT WRONG:

ANY REGRETS?

☐ YES NOPE ☐

TO BE READ UPON MY DEATH • CONFESSION 204

THE EXACT MOMENT THAT I KNEW THEY WERE 'THE ONE':

. . . .

. . . .

. . . .

. . . .

. . . .

ANY REGRETS?

☐ YES NOPE ☐

TO BE READ UPON MY DEATH • CONFESSION 205

THE EXACT MOMENT THAT I REALIZED I WAS HORRIBLY WRONG:

. . . .

. . . .

. . . .

. . . .

. . . .

ANY REGRETS?

☐ YES NOPE ☐

TO BE READ UPON MY DEATH • CONFESSION 206

THE FIRST TIME I HAD TO GO UP ON A STAGE (AND HOW I MANAGED TO NOT THROW UP):

ANY REGRETS?

☐ YES

NOPE ☐

TO BE READ UPON MY DEATH • CONFESSION 207

THE ONLY CORRECT WAY TO CUT A SANDWICH (ACCORDING TO ME):

ANY REGRETS?

☐ YES

NOPE ☐

WHO I PLAN TO HAUNT AND WHY:

ANY REGRETS?

☐ YES NOPE ☐

EXHIBIT A

THE SICKEST I HAVE EVER BEEN WAS...

ANY REGRETS?

☐ YES NOPE ☐

EXHIBIT A

TO BE READ UPON MY DEATH • CONFESSION 210

THAT TIME I MADE IT ON THE NEWS:

ANY REGRETS?

☐ YES NOPE ☐

TO BE READ UPON MY DEATH • CONFESSION 211

I DON'T CARE WHAT ANYONE ELSE SAYS, THE BEST BATMAN WAS OBVIOUSLY:

ANY REGRETS?

☐ YES NOPE ☐

TO BE READ UPON MY DEATH • CONFESSION 212

MY STANCE ON HARD VS. SOFT TACOS:

ANY REGRETS?

☐ YES NOPE ☐

TO BE READ UPON MY DEATH • CONFESSION 213

IF MY LIFE WAS A REALITY TELEVISION SERIES, IT WOULD MOST LIKELY AIR ON...

ANY REGRETS?

☐ YES NOPE ☐

TO BE READ UPON MY DEATH • CONFESSION 214

THE BEST BIRTHDAY I EVER HAD WAS...

ANY REGRETS?

☐ YES NOPE ☐

TO BE READ UPON MY DEATH • CONFESSION 215

MY MOST CONTROVERSIAL OPINION IS:

ANY REGRETS?

☐ YES NOPE ☐

TO BE READ UPON MY DEATH • CONFESSION 216

THE ONLY CONDIMENTS THAT SHOULD BE ALLOWED ON HOT DOGS (AND WHY EVERYONE ELSE IS A MONSTER):

ANY REGRETS?

☐ YES NOPE ☐

TO BE READ UPON MY DEATH • CONFESSION 217

THE BIGGEST FIGHT I'VE EVER HAD THAT DIRECTLY INVOLVED A BOARD GAME:

ANY REGRETS?

☐ YES NOPE ☐

THE TIME I WAS CALLED FOR JURY DUTY:

ANY REGRETS?

☐ YES NOPE ☐

EXHIBIT A

THE MOST ELABORATE AND CONVOLUTED LIE THAT I EVER TOLD WAS...

ANY REGRETS?

☐ YES

NOPE ☐

EXHIBIT A

TO BE READ UPON MY DEATH • CONFESSION 220

WHY THE PROM IS OVERRATED:

ANY REGRETS?

☐ YES NOPE ☐

TO BE READ UPON MY DEATH • CONFESSION 221

WHY THE AFTER-PARTY IS OVERRATED:

ANY REGRETS?

☐ YES NOPE ☐

TO BE READ UPON MY DEATH • CONFESSION 222

I'M SURPRISED I'M STILL ALIVE AFTER...

ANY REGRETS?

☐ YES NOPE ☐

TO BE READ UPON MY DEATH • CONFESSION 223

THE ONE MOMENT IN COLLEGE I WOULD RELIVE (IF I HAD A MAGICAL TIME-TRAVELING HOT TUB):

ANY REGRETS?

☐ YES NOPE ☐

TO BE READ UPON MY DEATH • CONFESSION 224

THE FIRST FICTIONAL CHARACTER THAT I HAD A CRUSH ON WAS:

ANY REGRETS?

☐ YES NOPE ☐

TO BE READ UPON MY DEATH • CONFESSION 225

I SHOULD HAVE KEPT MY MOUTH SHUT:

ANY REGRETS?

☐ YES NOPE ☐

TO BE READ UPON MY DEATH • CONFESSION 226

THE ONE WHO GOT AWAY:

ANY REGRETS?

☐ YES NOPE ☐

TO BE READ UPON MY DEATH • CONFESSION 227

THE ONE I WISH HAD GOTTEN AWAY:

ANY REGRETS?

☐ YES NOPE ☐

MY FAVORITE TOY FROM CHILDHOOD WAS...

ANY REGRETS?

☐ YES

NOPE ☐

EXHIBIT A

TO BE READ UPON MY DEATH • CONFESSION 229

THE TIME I PRETENDED TO BE SOMEONE ELSE:

ANY REGRETS?

☐ YES NOPE ☐

TO BE READ UPON MY DEATH • CONFESSION 230

THE ONE MISSED PHOTO OPPORTUNITY THAT I WILL FOREVER REGRET:

ANY REGRETS?

☐ YES NOPE ☐

TO BE READ UPON MY DEATH • CONFESSION 231

IF I'M REINCARNATED, I CAN ONLY HOPE THAT I'LL COME BACK AS A...

. . . .

. . . .

. . . .

. . . .

. . . .

ANY REGRETS?

☐ YES NOPE ☐

TO BE READ UPON MY DEATH • CONFESSION 232

THE WEIRDEST DATE I EVER WENT ON:

. . . .

. . . .

. . . .

. . . .

. . . .

. . . .

ANY REGRETS?

☐ YES NOPE ☐

I REALLY COULDN'T HAVE BROKEN DOWN IN A WORSE LOCATION:

ANY REGRETS?

☐ YES NOPE ☐

EXHIBIT A

I KNEW THAT IT HAD TO BE TOO GOOD TO BE TRUE (AND WHY I WAS RIGHT):

ANY REGRETS?

☐ YES NOPE ☐

TO BE READ UPON MY DEATH • CONFESSION 235

THE MOST EMBARRASSING THING THAT I USED TO LOVE (AND STILL MAKES ME CRINGE A LITTLE):

ANY REGRETS?

☐ YES NOPE ☐

TO BE READ UPON MY DEATH • CONFESSION 236

THE NUMBER OF TIMES THAT MY HIGH SCHOOL G.P.A. HAS AFFECTED MY LIFE (AND WHY THE ANSWER IS ZERO):

ANY REGRETS?

☐ YES NOPE ☐

JUST IN CASE YOU WERE ON THE FENCE, HERE'S WHY YOU PROBABLY SHOULDN'T FALL ASLEEP ON THE SUBWAY:

ANY REGRETS?

☐ YES NOPE ☐

EXHIBIT A

HOW I MANAGED TO NEVER TAKE A SIP OF ALCOHOL UNTIL I TURNED 21 (JK, NOT REALLY):

ANY REGRETS?

☐ YES

NOPE ☐

TO BE READ UPON MY DEATH • CONFESSION 239

A CAUTIONARY TALE ABOUT CAR INSURANCE:

ANY REGRETS?

☐ YES NOPE ☐

TO BE READ UPON MY DEATH • CONFESSION 240

MY BIGGEST CELEBRITY CRUSH HAS ALWAYS BEEN (AND WILL ALWAYS BE):

ANY REGRETS?

☐ YES NOPE ☐

TO BE READ UPON MY DEATH • CONFESSION 241

IN HINDSIGHT, THAT APARTMENT WAS AWFUL AND CERTAINLY NOT UP TO CODE:

ANY REGRETS?

☐ YES NOPE ☐

TO BE READ UPON MY DEATH • CONFESSION 242

THE WORST FIRST IMPRESSION I EVER MADE:

ANY REGRETS?

☐ YES NOPE ☐

TO BE READ UPON MY DEATH • CONFESSION 243

THE TIME THAT I PUT 'NEVER-ENDING BREAD STICKS' TO THE TEST:

ANY REGRETS?

☐ YES NOPE ☐

TO BE READ UPON MY DEATH • CONFESSION 244

THE WEIRDEST ROOMMATE I EVER HAD WAS...

ANY REGRETS?

☐ YES NOPE ☐

TO BE READ UPON MY DEATH • CONFESSION 245

I'M 100% CONFIDENT THAT I COULD WIN AN EATING COMPETITION—AS LONG AS THE FOOD WAS...

ANY REGRETS?

☐ YES NOPE ☐

TO BE READ UPON MY DEATH • CONFESSION 246

THE BEST MOVIE EVER MADE (ACCORDING TO ME):

ANY REGRETS?

☐ YES NOPE ☐

THE DAY I MET MY BEST FRIEND:

ANY REGRETS?

☐ YES

NOPE ☐

EXHIBIT A

THAT TIME I HUNG OUT WITH A CELEBRITY:

ANY REGRETS?

☐ YES

NOPE ☐

EXHIBIT A

TO BE READ UPON MY DEATH • CONFESSION 249

I HATE THINKING ABOUT IT, BUT THE WORDS I MOST WISH I COULD TAKE BACK ARE...

ANY REGRETS?

☐ YES NOPE ☐

TO BE READ UPON MY DEATH • CONFESSION 250

IN MY DEFENSE, I DIDN'T KNOW THAT I WAS CONTAGIOUS:

ANY REGRETS?

☐ YES NOPE ☐

TO BE READ UPON MY DEATH • CONFESSION 251

AS IT TURNS OUT, THE DOOR WASN'T ACTUALLY LOCKED...

ANY REGRETS?

☐ YES NOPE ☐

TO BE READ UPON MY DEATH • CONFESSION 252

I DIDN'T EVEN KNOW IT WAS POSSIBLE TO BE IN THAT MUCH PAIN:

ANY REGRETS?

☐ YES NOPE ☐

TO BE READ UPON MY DEATH • CONFESSION 253

THE TIME THAT I TRIED (AND FAILED) TO DRIVE ALL NIGHT WITHOUT TAKING A BREAK:

ANY REGRETS?

☐ YES

NOPE ☐

TO BE READ UPON MY DEATH • CONFESSION 254

I WILL FOREVER STAND BY THIS WEIRD (BUT AMAZING) FOOD COMBINATION:

ANY REGRETS?

☐ YES

☐

TO BE READ UPON MY DEATH • CONFESSION 255

MY PERSONAL BELIEFS IN REGARDS TO NAPPING (AND HOW THEY'VE EVOLVED THE OLDER I GET):

....

....

....

....

....

ANY REGRETS?

☐ YES NOPE ☐

TO BE READ UPON MY DEATH • CONFESSION 256

IT'S PROBABLY TOO LATE NOW, BUT I STILL OWE THEM AN APOLOGY:

....

....

....

....

....

ANY REGRETS?

☐ YES NOPE ☐

A CAUTIONARY TALE ABOUT ONLINE DATING:

ANY REGRETS?

☐ YES NOPE ☐

EXHIBIT A

THAT ONE TIME THAT I LEGITIMATELY TRIED TO RUN AWAY FROM HOME (AND HOW FAR I ACTUALLY GOT):

ANY REGRETS?

☐ YES NOPE ☐

EXHIBIT A

TO BE READ UPON MY DEATH • CONFESSION 259

IT WAS ALL JUST A BIG MISUNDERSTANDING:

ANY REGRETS?

☐ YES NOPE ☐

TO BE READ UPON MY DEATH • CONFESSION 260

AS IT TURNS OUT, HOSTELS ARE ABOUT AS ENJOYABLE AS THEY SOUND:

ANY REGRETS?

☐ YES NOPE ☐

TO BE READ UPON MY DEATH • CONFESSION 261

MY STANCE ON NIGHT VS. MORNING SHOWERS:

ANY REGRETS?

☐ YES NOPE ☐

TO BE READ UPON MY DEATH • CONFESSION 262

DESPITE NOT GETTING THE FULL RECOGNITION THAT I DESERVED, MY GREATEST TRIUMPH WAS...

ANY REGRETS?

☐ YES NOPE ☐

TO BE READ UPON MY DEATH • CONFESSION 263

IN CASE YOU WERE WONDERING, THE PEOPLE IN CUSTOMS TAKE BODY SEARCHES VERY SERIOUSLY:

ANY REGRETS?

☐ YES

NOPE ☐

TO BE READ UPON MY DEATH • CONFESSION 264

HERE'S WHY YOU SHOULD ALWAYS TIP:

ANY REGRETS?

☐ YES

NOPE ☐

TO BE READ UPON MY DEATH • CONFESSION 265

THE POLICE TOTALLY DIDN'T BELIEVE ME (AND YOU PROBABLY WON'T EITHER) BUT...

ANY REGRETS?

☐ YES NOPE ☐

TO BE READ UPON MY DEATH • CONFESSION 266

THE ONE SOUND THAT I'LL ALWAYS HATE:

ANY REGRETS?

☐ YES NOPE ☐

THE MOST REGRETTABLE HAIRCUT OF MY LIFE:

ANY REGRETS?

☐ YES

NOPE ☐

EXHIBIT A

IN HINDSIGHT, I SHOULD HAVE BECOME A...

ANY REGRETS?

☐ YES

NOPE ☐

EXHIBIT A

TO BE READ UPON MY DEATH • CONFESSION 269

I'LL PROBABLY REGRET THIS LATER, BUT MY CHILDHOOD NICKNAME WAS:

ANY REGRETS?

☐ YES NOPE ☐

TO BE READ UPON MY DEATH • CONFESSION 270

THAT ONE TIME I ACTUALLY (SUCCESSFULLY) TALKED MY WAY OUT OF A SPEEDING TICKET:

ANY REGRETS?

☐ YES NOPE ☐

TO BE READ UPON MY DEATH • CONFESSION 271

THE MOST HUNGOVER I'VE EVER BEEN:

ANY REGRETS?

☐ YES NOPE ☐

TO BE READ UPON MY DEATH • CONFESSION 272

MY STANCE ON DILL VS. SWEET PICKLES (AND WHY ONE OF THEM MAY OR MAY NOT BE THE SPAWN OF SATAN):

ANY REGRETS?

☐ YES NOPE ☐

TO BE READ UPON MY DEATH • CONFESSION 273

NOTHING IS MORE OVERRATED THAN:

ANY REGRETS?

☐ YES NOPE ☐

TO BE READ UPON MY DEATH • CONFESSION 274

NOTHING IS MORE UNDERRATED THAN:

ANY REGRETS?

☐ YES NOPE ☐

TO BE READ UPON MY DEATH • CONFESSION 275

THE MOST EMBARRASSING THING THAT I'VE EVER HAD TO TELL A DOCTOR:

ANY REGRETS?

☐ YES NOPE ☐

TO BE READ UPON MY DEATH • CONFESSION 276

THE FIRST BIRTHDAY PARTY THAT I CAN ACTUALLY REMEMBER:

ANY REGRETS?

☐ YES NOPE ☐

TO BE READ UPON MY DEATH • CONFESSION 277

I'VE NEVER LAUGHED HARDER THAN...

ANY REGRETS?

☐ YES NOPE ☐

EXHIBIT A

SEVERAL (HUNDRED) REASONS WHY BEING AN ADULT IS OVERRATED:

ANY REGRETS?

☐ YES NOPE ☐

EXHIBIT A

TO BE READ UPON MY DEATH • CONFESSION 279

THINGS YOU SHOULD NEVER GOOGLE:

. . . .

. . . .

. . . .

. . . .

. . . .

. . . .

ANY REGRETS?

☐ YES NOPE ☐

TO BE READ UPON MY DEATH • CONFESSION 280

MY VERY FIRST PET (AND WHY THEY WERE LITERALLY AN ANGEL ON EARTH):

. . . .

. . . .

. . . .

. . . .

. . . .

ANY REGRETS?

☐ YES NOPE ☐

TO BE READ UPON MY DEATH • CONFESSION 281

THE BEST VACATION THAT I EVER HAD WAS...

ANY REGRETS?

☐ YES NOPE ☐

TO BE READ UPON MY DEATH • CONFESSION 282

SPOILER ALERT: KIDS CAN BE ANNOYING (EVEN IF THEY'RE YOUR OWN):

ANY REGRETS?

☐ YES NOPE ☐

TO BE READ UPON MY DEATH • CONFESSION 283

MY STANCE ON CARRYING LUGGAGE ONTO A PLANE (AND WHY I'M CORRECT):

ANY REGRETS?

☐ YES NOPE ☐

TO BE READ UPON MY DEATH • CONFESSION 284

WHY YOU SHOULD LEARN TO CHANGE A TIRE:

ANY REGRETS?

☐ YES NOPE ☐

TO BE READ UPON MY DEATH • CONFESSION 285

HOW I'VE LITERALLY NEVER DONE ANYTHING EVEN REMOTELY WRONG, EVER (JK, NOT REALLY):

ANY REGRETS?

☐ YES NOPE ☐

TO BE READ UPON MY DEATH • CONFESSION 286

HOW BRASS MONKEY CHANGED MY LIFE:

ANY REGRETS?

☐ YES NOPE ☐

THINK YOU CAN DO BETTER? LET'S SEE IT. NOW IT'S YOUR TURN TO TELL YOUR OWN DEEP DARK SECRETS.

DON'T STOP WITH ONE. USE THE NEXT FEW PAGES TOO.

ANY REGRETS?

☐ YES NOPE ☐

TO BE READ UPON MY DEATH • BYO CONFESSION

ANY REGRETS?

☐ YES NOPE ☐

TO BE READ UPON MY DEATH • BYO CONFESSION

ANY REGRETS?

☐ YES NOPE ☐

TO BE READ UPON MY DEATH • BYO CONFESSION

ANY REGRETS?

☐ YES NOPE ☐

TO BE READ UPON MY DEATH • BYO CONFESSION

ANY REGRETS?

☐ YES NOPE ☐

TO BE READ UPON MY DEATH • BYO CONFESSION

ANY REGRETS?

☐ YES NOPE ☐

TO BE READ UPON MY DEATH • BYO CONFESSION

ANY REGRETS?

☐ YES NOPE ☐

TO BE READ UPON MY DEATH • BYO CONFESSION

ANY REGRETS?

☐ YES NOPE ☐

TO BE READ UPON MY DEATH • BYO CONFESSION

ANY REGRETS?

☐ YES NOPE ☐

TO BE READ UPON MY DEATH • BYO CONFESSION

ANY REGRETS?

☐ YES NOPE ☐

TO BE READ UPON MY DEATH • BYO CONFESSION

ANY REGRETS?

☐ YES NOPE ☐

TO BE READ UPON MY DEATH • BYO CONFESSION

ANY REGRETS?

☐ YES NOPE ☐

TO BE READ UPON MY DEATH • BYO CONFESSION

ANY REGRETS?

☐ YES NOPE ☐

TO BE READ UPON MY DEATH • BYO CONFESSION

ANY REGRETS?

☐ YES NOPE ☐

TO BE READ UPON MY DEATH • BYO CONFESSION

ANY REGRETS?

☐ YES NOPE ☐

TO BE READ UPON MY DEATH • BYO CONFESSION

ANY REGRETS?

☐ YES NOPE ☐

TO BE READ UPON MY DEATH • BYO CONFESSION

ANY REGRETS?

☐ YES NOPE ☐

TO BE READ UPON MY DEATH • BYO CONFESSION

ANY REGRETS?

☐ YES NOPE ☐

TO BE READ UPON MY DEATH • BYO CONFESSION

ANY REGRETS?

☐ YES NOPE ☐

TO BE READ UPON MY DEATH • BYO CONFESSION

ANY REGRETS?

☐ YES NOPE ☐

TO BE READ UPON MY DEATH • BYO CONFESSION

ANY REGRETS?

☐ YES NOPE ☐

TO BE READ UPON MY DEATH • BYO CONFESSION

ANY REGRETS?

☐ YES

NOPE ☐

TO BE READ UPON MY DEATH • BYO CONFESSION

ANY REGRETS?

☐ YES

NOPE ☐

TO BE READ UPON MY DEATH • BYO CONFESSION

ANY REGRETS?

☐ YES NOPE ☐

TO BE READ UPON MY DEATH • BYO CONFESSION

ANY REGRETS?

☐ YES NOPE ☐

TO BE READ UPON MY DEATH • BYO CONFESSION

ANY REGRETS?

☐ YES NOPE ☐

TO BE READ UPON MY DEATH • BYO CONFESSION

ANY REGRETS?

☐ YES NOPE ☐

TO BE READ UPON MY DEATH • BYO CONFESSION

ANY REGRETS?

☐ YES NOPE ☐

TO BE READ UPON MY DEATH • BYO CONFESSION

ANY REGRETS?

☐ YES NOPE ☐